ALIKE IN LOVE

ALIKE IN LOVE

When Opposites Attract

TIM & BEVERLY LAHAYE

New Leaf Press

TIM &
BEVERLY
LAHAYE

THE
HEARTH
AND
HOME
SERIES

First printing: March 1998

**Published in association with the literary
agency of Alive Communications, Inc., 1465
Kelly Johnson Blvd., Ste. 320, Colorado
Springs, CO 80920.**

ISBN: 0-89221-369-8
Library of Congress Number: 97-75864

Cover by Left Coast Design, Portland, OR.

Interior illustrations by Pamela Klenczar

Introduction

Bev and I had been married for 12 years before we were introduced to the four temperaments theory of why people act the way they do. Very honestly, those were our least happy years, because we couldn't understand why two people who loved each other could be so different.

By nature we are total opposites. She likes music, art, and culture. I am a sports nut. She loves to plan things in advance, I like spontaneity — "let nature take its course" is my motto. We constantly saw everything differently. By nature we collided on almost every decision.

When we found the temperament concept, we understood — she is a phlegmatic/sanguine/melancholy and I am a choleric/sanguine. Once we understood that, we were able to accept why we spontaneously responded to everything differently. Now we can almost anticipate each other's response and even laugh at things that once caused irritation and sometimes tension.

But this book is more than just explaining why you act the way you do and why the two of you are so opposite — it offers sound principles on how to adjust to your opposite partner. We think it can enrich and improve any couple's marriage.

Happy reading!

— Tim LaHaye

Alike in Love

A concerned mother phoned me from Arizona. "My daughter and son-in-law are having marital problems," she told me sadly. "They are currently visiting southern California. If they come to your city, will you see them?"

"Of course," I agreed. "Just have them call to set up a time."

Tuesday evening they arrived at my office, and almost immediately the wife informed me, "Our parents asked us to come to you. That's the only reason we're here."

Now there's a challenge for any marriage counselor.

"Besides, there's no hope for our marriage," the husband added. "Tomorrow we're returning home, and we have an appointment with our attorney on Thursday morning."

"Why are so you convinced it's hopeless?" I inquired.

"We've just returned from a counseling center, where we took a battery of psychological tests," the husband responded.

"The counselor concluded that we are hopelessly mismatched."

"What did he suggest?" I asked, knowing such tests are designed by psychologists who don't consider God's Word as the final authority.

"A divorce," the wife stated, dabbing her eyes with a tissue.

The husband looked at me. "What do you think?"

"I'm so glad you asked," I began. "That is the worst advice I've ever heard coming from a so-called Christian counselor."

Shocked, they both stared at me as I continued. "The Bible is very clear on the subject of divorce, is it not?" Neither partner answered.

"The Bible says if you're married, 'seek not to be loosed' — period!" I stated emphatically. "It doesn't take a theologian to figure that out."

"You mean we have to stay married and be miserable the rest of our lives?" the husband whined.

"No, just the first part," I answered with a smile.

I challenge anyone to find two marriage partners who are absolutely compatible in all areas. In fact, no two people on earth are alike. Differences are inevitable when a man and a woman decide to become one in a marriage relationship.

God doesn't expect Christian couples to stay married and be miserable. He wants you to be happy and has given instructions on how to live together in love and harmony.

Back in the first century — when God gave the commands "Husbands, love your wives" and "Wives, submit to your husbands" — most couples were married to partners their parents had selected for them. Young men and women married by faith and stayed married by obeying God.

"But my husband — or wife — is totally opposite from me!" you complain.

Is that grounds for divorce? After all, you chose your mate. Could it be that opposites really do attract one another? If so, then maybe there is a reason for this attraction.

Let me outline the advice I gave the couple who claimed they were "hopelessly mismatched."

How to Adjust to an Opposite Partner

My wife, Bev, and I are total opposites. If there are two

ways of doing anything, she will choose one and I will choose the other. It doesn't matter if it's disciplining children or buying food or paying bills or anything else, we just approach life differently.

Going to the airport on time has always created a lot of tension between us. I happen to believe there are only two minutes that count — the minute before and the minute after. I don't like to waste a lot of time at the airport.

Bev, on the other hand, insists on being there early. If the airline says an hour, she wants to arrive two hours before.

In spite of our different ways of doing things, Bev and I have a wonderful marriage. After all, it was those very differences that attracted us — as two college sweethearts — to one another. Over the years, we've come to realize that our opposite temperaments have actually worked to our advantage. How? We complement each other. Where she is weak, I am strong — and vice versa. Best of all, it has certainly made life interesting!

Temperament is only one part of our makeup; personality and character comprise the other two parts. Your personality — the way the you project yourself — is actually an outgrowth of your temperament. Character determines who you really are. Sometimes people project a good personality but have a bad character.

As a Christian, you should have "a transparent character." In other words, what you present as a personality should be your character; your personality and character should be one and the same.

Temperament is not personality. What is temperament? The involuntary cause of your actions and reactions that influences approximately 20 to 30 percent of your current behavior. Note the adjective "involuntary." That means it is beyond your control. In fact, your academic interests and vocational abilities often result from the makeup of your temperament.

Although you are born with a certain type of temperament, it can be adjusted and refined by the Holy Spirit and the principles you learn from the Word of God.

By identifying your own — and your mate's — temperament type, you will better understand yourself and your husband or wife.

Identify Yours — and Your Mate's — Temperament Type

Each temperament type has strengths and weaknesses. To simplify the four temperament types, we can separate them into two categories: the extroverts and the introverts.

Extroverts are easy to identify: They can't wait to interrupt the person who's talking so they can put in their two cents' worth. You know, "Enough about you; let's talk about me!"

Extroverts usually have a sanguine or a choleric temperament

Introverts, on the other hand, can outwait anyone. Easy-going and polite, they would never think of barging into a conversation.

The melancholics and the phlegmatics tend to have a more introverted type temperament.

Although Hippocrates is often considered the author of the temperament theory, King Solomon — 500 years before Hippocrates — wrote about four kinds of people in chapter 30 of the Book of Proverbs: melancholics, phlegmatics, sanguines, and cholerics.

The Melancholy Temperament

Proverbs 30:11 describes, in a symbolic way, people who are born with a melancholy temperament: "There is a generation that curses its father, And does not bless its mother."

While this verse does not literally apply to melancholics, it reflects how they generally feel and act toward people. They can find fault with anyone — themselves included.

Thinkers, analyzers, mystics, and musicians usually have a melancholy tempera-ment. These very ca-pable people, how-ever, are often terri-bly insecure. They don't like anybody or anything. In fact, they sometimes don't even like themselves.

The laid-back temperament of mel-ancholics, however,

makes them more gifted in areas that require a great degree of self-discipline and concentration. As a result, they develop their intellect and talents to perfection and are often scholars, artists, concert pianists, and chess players.

Mathematicians almost always have either a melancholy or phlegmatic temperament. You'll find that college professors have a high degree of melancholy because of their analytical capabilities. The sensitive, insecure nature of the melancholic, however, makes him prone to self-introspection and depression.

When a couple came to me for counseling one day, I could tell right away that she was the typical melancholy wife. Very exacting and perfectionist-oriented, she got right to the point. "I wish you would tell my husband that he's got to quit lying!" she blurted out. "He lies, lies, lies."

Since she had never confronted him about this issue before, he was shocked. "What do you mean I'm lying?" he asked quite perplexed.

I, too, wondered about the wife's accusation. I knew him to be a respected leader in his church and a happy-go-lucky sanguine kind of guy.

"You just lie all the time," she remarked, obviously upset.

"Give me an example," the husband demanded.

"Last night at the church party," she said, "I counted. You told 12 lies."

Astonished, he looked at her and said, "Well, they laughed, didn't they?" You see, sanguines tell stories for effect. Melancholics tell stories for accuracy.

A melancholic, when giving directions, is not content to say, "Well, you go out here, about three and a half miles until you find another road and you turn to the left." No, she will say, "Go three and four-tenth miles, and turn onto the first dirt road across from the large red barn with a black roof."

The Phlegmatic Temperament

The 12th verse of Proverbs 30 describes the nice people, the *phlegmatics*. They get along with everybody. "There is a generation that is pure in its own eyes, Yet is not washed from its filthiness." Phlegmatics are super introverts — quiet and diplomatic. Their motto is, "Still waters run deep." These easy-going types seldom get angry or irritated. Nothing ruffles them, and they seem to just float through life. They can come to church for four hours

— attend Bible class, worship the Lord during the morning service — and leave without saying little more than "Good morning" and "Goodbye" to a few people.

If you ask him how he's doing, he will answer, "Fine."

It's not that they are against talk; they just don't do it. Maybe it takes too much energy.

I like to be around phlegmatics because they have a great sense of humor. Since they don't like for anyone to be upset, they make jokes to diffuse unpleasant situations.

Some of the best counselors are phlegmatics because they like to listen to people and tend to be very objective. Their practical, utilitarian, and diplomatic approach to life often succeeds in bringing opposing parties together.

These low-key introverts, however, are not perfect. Their biggest problem is motivation — they don't have any. From the time they are born, their inertia level starts running down. As they grow older, they get slower and slower.

If you get them up, keep them moving. If they sit down, they'll relax; and if they relax, they'll fall asleep.

They are masters at procrastination and live by the motto "Always put off until tomorrow." That could be the reason phlegmatics are so indecisive and frequently vacillating between two opinions.

Phlegmatics can spend 30 minutes to an hour every morning getting organized to go to school or work. Then at the end of the day they get organized to go home. They probably do five hours worth of work in an eight-hour day. Phlegmatics love details and precision, which makes them great engineers and math teachers. In fact, these compulsive neat-nicks will organize anything that's not nailed down.

After one of my seminars on this subject, a wife came up to me and said, "When you were talking abut the characteristics of a phlegmatic, you were describing my husband to a tee. He not only has all his shirts in one section and all his pants in another and his sweaters and suits very well-organized, he even has his shirts hung by color so that he can pick out the one he needs without disturbing the others."

Phlegmatics are also very conservative. Unfortunately, they conserve everything — even their love. Underneath their nice, gentle spirit, they can be very selfish, self-protecting individuals.

They don't like to give too much of their love — or themselves — because they might be hurt.

As natural born worriers they are plagued by fear, worry, and anxiety. This could be why they are prone to be frugal and stingy with money. They have to learn to be generous.

On the positive side, phlegmatics often exhibit more Christ-like behavior before they become Christians than the rest of us do afterward. They are wonderful people if they can get their emotions under control.

The teenage children of a Jewish doctor were saved in our youth program. The dramatic change in their lives so impressed their dad that he agreed to allow his wife to attend church. When she got saved, he said, "Something's going on over there," and started coming on Sunday mornings.

After several weeks, I had the opportunity to share the gospel with him and present Jesus Christ as the Messiah and Saviour of the world. The doctor looked me straight in the eye and said, "Pastor LaHaye, that's a beautiful story, and I believe it, but I don't think I need it."

I was stunned.

"I'm a nice person," he told me, "and a good citizen. I don't overcharge my patients, and if they get into financial trouble, I just write it off. Of course, I do meet a lot of people who need what you're talking about, but I don't think I need it."

Many phlegmatics are such naturally nice people that they don't view themselves as sinners.

It took two years for this man to realize that he — like all of us — had sinned and "fallen short of the glory of God." When he finally understood that, this good doctor received Christ.

The Sanguine Temperament

The two extrovert temperaments are the *sanguine* (the super extrovert) and the *choleric* (the managerial type).

Verse 13 of Proverbs 30 describes this third temperament: the *sanguine*. "There is a generation — oh, how lofty are their eyes! And their eyelids are lifted up."

Sanguines are constantly looking around. Why? Because their focus is always, "Where is my audience?"

These attention-seeking, fast-talking, super-extroverts have charisma to burn. With a tendency to stretch the truth, sanguines like to exaggerate to make a point or add punch to the punch line.

If you have ever bought a used car, the salesman was probably a sanguine. Who else could sell a pile of junk and call it a car? These wonderful, friendly types relate well to everyone they meet and are great at public relations.

If you want someone to communicate with — actually you'll mostly just listen — get a sanguine. You may have to tell him *what* to communicate, but he can communicate better than anyone I know. They have so much charm, you want to do whatever they say even though you don't want to do it. That's the effect they have on people.

Sanguines, on the other hand, are generally not academically inclined; they focus on people and find it difficult to concentrate for long periods of time. Sanguines and cholerics usually don't excel at math or spelling, but they do well in history and political science.

Like all the temperament types, sanguines have some serious weaknesses. Although they have tremendous charisma and ability, they lack self-discipline and have a hard time channeling their efforts in the right direction.

Oddly enough, sanguines are very compassionate. If you want a doctor with a good bedside manner, always go to Dr. Sanguine. When he comes into the hospital room where you are lying pale as a ghost and on the verge of death, his eyes are full of concern. Dr. Sanguine walks over, takes your hand, and rubs it.

Your heart begins to palpitate, blood comes back into your face, and you appear to be alive. Then out the door he goes! He forgets to look at your chart because sanguines are careless about details . . . and you die. Don't feel bad — all his patients die happy.

The Choleric Temperament

Verse 14 of Proverbs 30 describes the *choleric* person: "There is a generation whose teeth are like swords, And whose fangs are like knives, To devour the poor from off the earth, And the needy from among men."

This character is tough and determined — the master sergeant type. He wants to be in charge of every situation. When he sets his jaw to do something, nothing can dissuade him.

Before he was even two years old, my grandson was already exhibiting his choleric temperament. One day I noticed he was struggling to put on his little tennis shoes, so I said, "Joel, let me help you."

He pushed my hand away and said, "I can do it myself."

No one can teach a toddler to be stubborn. That's born in a child. Joel didn't know how to tie his shoes, but he was determined to do it himself. "He'll probably grow up to be very successful," I told Bev, "if he doesn't self-destruct beforehand!"

This dominating, dictator-type personality knows how to order people around and guide them through life. Saddam Hussein is probably a choleric. This type of person thrives on opposition. If you say, "You can't do that!" they say, "Watch me!"

The modus operandi of the choleric is usually "the end justifies the means." They do whatever they think is expedient. If their actions are questioned, they simply try to justify themselves. Cholerics are visionaries. They are constantly making goals and dreaming dreams, yet they sometimes have trouble putting their plans into action.

Not a perfectionist by nature, the extro-

vert choleric does tend to be well-organized, practical, and utilitarian. Since they are also very productive, they are prone to become workaholics. A choleric husband will tell his wife, "I am away so much because I work long and hard so I can make things better for you and the kids." The truth is they love to work. Cholerics are also very decisive. They don't vacillate between two decisions. When they make up their mind, they do it. They're what business calls SNL's — strong, natural leaders.

Along with all these good traits come some serious weaknesses. One is lack of emotion. They're not affectionate people and can actually be cold and indifferent.

I've had sanguine men or melancholy men who are married to choleric women say, "My wife is so cold."

"Don't worry," I tell them. "It's not that she's frigid; it's just

that she thinks kissing can spread germs."

This attitude reflects their cut and dry approach to life — a quality that also makes cholerics very self-sufficient. "I can do very well by myself, thank you," is their attitude. Since they don't like to beat around the bush, they can quickly cut a person down to size with their sarcastic tongue.

Further on the down side, they are impetuous, domineering, and unforgiving. You get one strike in their ball game and, "That's it! I trusted you 35 years ago, and you failed me! Don't think I have forgotten!"

Face the Fact That Opposites Attract

Two people of the same temperament type almost never get married. Why? Because like temperaments repel, they don't attract.

Two sanguines would never get married. They might date for a while, but their relationship would be so emotionally supercharged it wouldn't last. Besides, one of them would have to stop talking long enough to listen — and that would never happen. Eventually, they would get bored because, as Shakespeare said to the sanguine, "All the world's a stage." Who wants to be a performer without an audience? Both would be vying for center stage, and that never works.

Two cholerics would rarely marry. In fact, they would rarely go out together unless someone else arranged a blind date. Even then they would get into a fight before they got to the car. Where are we going? Who's going to drive? Who's going to pay? They would be home in an hour.

Two phlegmatics might date. They'd go together, go together, and go together, but they'd both die of old age before one got up enough steam to ask the other one to marry.

Two melancholics could date for a while since their temperament spectrum has a broad range. In a sadistic mood, they might even decide to marry each other — but it's not very likely.

As a general rule, opposites tend to attract each other. Sparky Sanguine is usually attracted to Melanie Melancholy. When he looks at her, he thinks, *This chick has really got her act together!*

He's right. Her eye shadow matches the patent leather on her shoes, which matches the little purse placed neatly on her lap. Every hair lies sprayed into place, and her nails are manicured to perfection.

Sparky, on the other hand, is totally disorganized. Any time

you see a sanguine who is color-coordinated, his wife (or his mother) picked out his clothes. He's usually wearing striped slacks with a plaid shirt and a paisley tie — topped off with a wild jacket. He never wears dull colors because his whole goal in life is to be noticed.

Sparky's outgoing — sometimes obnoxious — ways, however, appeal to Melanie who herself longs to be an uninhibited, free spirit. She can't, of course, because her temperament won't let her. Yet, it is Melanie's quiet, sensitive demeanor that draws Sparky to her side. After all, she makes the perfect captive audience. She laughs at all his jokes and never interrupts his self-centered monologues. Eventually, Sparky and Melanie get married.

You can imagine what happens next. Every item sloppy Sparky puts down, neat Melanie wants him to pick up. "Be sure to put all your clothes away."

"Okay," he replies and opens his closet door as everything falls out.

After Sparky goes to work in the morning, Melanie goes back into the bathroom to find he's used everything and put nothing away.

Is this couple going to have a period of adjustment? You better believe it.

If you simply decide to endure one another and say, "Well, I'm going to tough it out because we promised to stay together until death do us part," you will find it gets tougher and tougher through the years. Only when the Holy Spirit of God fills your life will you have the resources to blend the two of you together — and live happily ever after.

Why do opposites attract each other? Why wouldn't two cholerics get together? Why wouldn't two phlegmatics marry? Wouldn't it be simpler if you had two organized people living together? No. Your marriage needs the strengths of the other temperament to make it work.

After years of struggling to manage our family finances, I finally admitted: I'm a terrible bookkeeper. When balancing the family checkbook my motto was: Who cares as long as it's close?

I used to keep a pair of bank accounts. For about four months, I would write checks on one account until all the checks came in on the other account. Then I would use the second account until the first one settled and I had some idea of how much money I had left. Over the course of a year it never cost me more than $10

or $12! Besides, one account was always within four months of being accurate.

One day as Bev and I were walking through the bank, the banker — who was a friend of ours — called my wife over and said, "Mrs. LaHaye, would it be possible to get your husband to turn the bookkeeping over to you?"

That night, we had a "honey" talk, and I agreed that she should take over keeping the checking account balanced.

About two months later I found her sitting at the dining room table worriedly shifting through a pile of checks. After about three hours, I finally asked, "Honey, what are you doing?"

Without glancing up, she said, "I'm looking for ten cents."

Ten cents? "Here, I'll give you ten cents!" I shouted in amazement. "Stop wasting your time!

"No," she replied emphatically. "I can't quit until I find it!"

Since I understand her temperament, I didn't argue. I knew that's the way she's wired.

And finally she found the ten missing pennies.

Details intrigue her. Bev will get up in the morning and do a crossword puzzle. I've never done a crossword puzzle in my whole life, and I have no desire or interest ever to do one.

We have different temperaments. Since we are aware of our different strengths and weaknesses, I don't try to make her like me, and she accepts me for what I am. We respect our differences.

Once you realize, "That's the way he, or she, is," back off. Stop trying to change your mate. That's how God created him or her. The sooner you accept your differences, the better your marriage will be.

Admit to Yourself, "I'm Not Perfect"

We are all subconsciously attracted to someone who is strong where we are weak. You're not attracted to a person who has the same weaknesses as yours. Why? Because you hate your own weaknesses. That's natural.

When you see someone who is strong where you are weak, you become infatuated. You enjoy spending time with that person. Infatuation leads to admiration, and admiration leads to association. Association can lead to love and, hopefully, love leads to marriage.

Since temperament spontaneously influences almost everything we do, it not only affects where our strengths lie but determines our weaknesses. The way a person drives a car depends on his temperament.

Cholerics drive in and out of lanes and take every shortcut in an effort to save a minute going to church or to work.

Sanguines are often dangerous drivers because they are so people-oriented. If you sit in the front, it's okay. If you sit in the back, he'll be turning around to talk to you — and that can be hazardous to your health.

Melancholics drive exactly right. I mean, they rarely get tickets, they always drive one mile under the speed limit — never over the speed limit. And everything is perfect.

Phlegmatics drive about 15 miles under the speed limit and come to a complete stop before entering the on-ramp of the freeway, creating a long line of traffic behind them. Phlegmatics never get into accidents; they cause them.

How about shopping? I can immediately identify a person's temperament by the way he or she browses at my book table.

Sanguines look at my book table and say, "Oh, these are beautiful. I want one of everything." They buy them all but never read them.

The choleric comes up to the book table and says to her husband, "You need to read this, and you need that, and you need the other one."

The melancholic comes up, looks over the selections very carefully, picks up a book then puts it down. Later, he comes back and looks at it again and puts it down.

Phlegmatics don't buy many books; they usually fall asleep reading.

Temperament also determines our eating habits. Sanguines are often overweight for two reasons: They have no self-discipline, and they eat too fast. Since sanguines do everything fast, they gulp down their meals in 10 minutes. They gain weight because it takes 20 minutes for food to enter your stomach and shut off your hunger pangs. By that time, a sanguine has had two meals! Then he feels over-stuffed and has to swallow a roll of Tums.

The choleric, who must always be busy doing something, gains weight because he likes the oral satisfaction of chewing.

The melancholic, however, never eats anything without

analyzing the fine print to decode the calorie content, the nutritional value, and the presence of any additives that may have an adverse chemical effect on the environment — particularly his.

The phlegmatics almost never get fat. Why? They eat very slowly and often stop before they finish the entire meal. A phlegmatic child should never be forced to clean his plate. Let him eat what he wants at meals, but avoid snacks in between.

Our emotional makeup and the way we react to people and situations comes from our temperament.

When the sanguine gets mad, he blows up quickly, rakes you over the coals, and then forgets all about it. He never carries a grudge and never gets ulcers — he just gives them to everybody else.

The choleric is also quick to get angry, but he has a hard time letting go of it. He or she tends to harbor resentment, and by the time the choleric is 48 years old — unless he allows the

Holy Spirit to change him — he'll either be a Rolaids addict or on his way to the grave.

Your handwriting also serves as a dead giveaway of your temperament. If you have a big, flowing style, your temperament is probably big and flowing. If you write little scribbly letters that hardly anyone can read, that's an outgrowth of your temperament.

By now, you have probably found yourself in one of these temperaments — or you may have identified traits from one or more. Actually, most people have a primary temperament and a secondary temperament. For an accurate and detailed analysis of your temperament, send for the LaHaye Temperament Analysis described in the back of this book.

I have never met a 100 percent sanguine person. If he existed, he would sell the earth! Nor have I encountered an individual who is 100 percent choleric (he would probably run the earth).

Imagine a man who has a primary temperament that is 60 percent sanguine and a secondary temperament of 40 percent choleric. Look out! This "san-clor" would be a super-extroverted leader.

How about a "san-mel" — a sanguine/melancholic? She would be a highly emotional person prone to cry at telephone numbers and birds that fly overhead.

A "san-phleg" — a sanguine/phlegmatic — would be a self-indulgent, happy floater who would sink into bankruptcy by the time he was 40 years of age. A nice person, but not very productive.

Suppose someone's primary temperament is 60 percent choleric and 40 percent sanguine. That would create a "clor-san" — an extroverted, highly energetic leader and producer.

The two worst workaholics are the cholerics and the melancholic. A 60-40 "clor-mel" would always be crusading for some cause or trying to change something and make it better.

The "clor-phleg" — a 60-40 choleric phlegmatic would make a great administrator. Gentle and diplomatic because of the phlegmatic, he would be forceful enough to supervise people without dominating them.

A 60-40 "mel-san" would make a great teacher because the sanguine has the ability to say it, and the melancholy has something to say. If we turned it around, however, we might get a teacher who talks too much about nothing.

The "mel-clor" person makes a gifted medical doctor. In fact, I am not sure a doctor could get through medical school without some melancholy. This part of his temperament provides him with a high IQ and the ability to look at words and remember them.

A person who is 60 percent phlegmatic and 40 percent sanguine makes for a very congenial, people-oriented individual who is often medical or service oriented.

The "phleg-clor" has great leadership potential and makes a good administrator.

The "phleg-mel" creates a superb scholar who wouldn't be an irritator.

As you find yourself and your mate in one or more of these

categories, the realization has probably dawned that you have weaknesses, too. After all, your mate has pointed them out many times! Cut yourself a break and admit, "I'm not perfect, either." It will do wonders for your own self-esteem and set you free from unrealistic expectations.

Always remember, God is not finished with you yet. He has given you His Holy Spirit to strengthen your weaknesses.

Accept Your Partner's Temperament

Don't conflict with your partner's temperament. If your partner is a sanguine, expect him or her to be loud, self-centered, and seemingly arrogant. Of course, this kind of behavior varies by degrees, but a sanguine will never be a phlegmatic.

Your mate cannot change his in-born temperament. That means the ball is in your court. It's up to you to understand why your mate acts that way and work with it. You married him or her. Something about his temperament type must have appealed to you in the beginning. Now you need to accept it by giving thanks to God.

A dear friend of ours — a well-known author whose name you would recognize — told us an amusing story about her marriage. A lovely sanguine, this lady is outgoing, bubbly, and writes Christian books. Her husband is just the opposite; he is a melancholy accountant and banker.

One day she shared with me how my little book, *Spirit Controlled Temperament,* was used by God in their lives.

Nothing irritated her more than the way her husband always checked up on her. She described how they would crawl into bed at night, and he'd put his big, brawny arm under her neck. As she snuggled next to him, she would find herself responding to his rather amorous mood. Then all of a sudden, he'd stop and call her by name, and say, "Did you lock the back door?"

That question didn't bother her because locking the door was her responsibility. She'd reply, "Yes, I did."

Suddenly, he would jerk his arm out from under her neck, leap out of bed, run through the dining room into the kitchen, and check the back door. By then, she was fuming! What a put-down! His actions indicated he didn't trust her. By the time he came back to bed, you can be sure he was crawling in with an iceberg.

The next night, they repeated the same charade. She would

start to respond to his mood, and all of a sudden he'd say, "Honey, did you lock the back door?" And sure enough, he'd race and check it.

As she read my book on the different temperament types, she realized her husband was a melancholy. As an accountant, he focused on precision in everything he did. It takes a melancholy to be a successful accountant. In fact, I've never met a sanguine accountant who made any money. He could sell the service for someone else, but he would never have the self-discipline to sit for hours checking and rechecking numbers on balance sheets.

That night she walked through the dining room where her husband was working on a client's tax return. This was years ago — before calculators and computers. She watched as he went down the 1040 form, adding up a column of figures. Then he took a little scrap of paper and wrote down his answer, turned it over and went down the same column and added them again, wrote it down and turned it over. Then he started at the bottom, went up, wrote it down, turned it over, and came down again — four times.

Her husband didn't know she was watching, but as he turned the first piece of paper over, he smiled. Then the second one. His smile got bigger and bigger and bigger as all four figures were the same. Since they all agreed, he wrote the final number at the bottom of the form.

Then she suddenly realized! "He doesn't just check up on me, he checks up on himself!"

A perfectionist doesn't only expect perfection from his mate. He is as critical of himself as he is of you.

That night she was ready for him. He put his arm under her neck, and she responded to him, Then at the crucial moment, he asked, "Did you lock the back door?" And she said, "Yes, I did, honey, but if you want to check it, go ahead." And sure enough, he did.

She was different that night when he came back to bed because she understood his temperament. The temperament theory helps you understand your partner so you can work with him or her to create harmony in your relationship.

Focus on Your Mate's Strengths

When you face the fact that you are not perfect, you can accept the fact that your partner isn't perfect, either. Your partner

has weaknesses. When opposite temperament types marry, their strengths and weaknesses are also opposite. A partner who is strong in one area can't understand why his or her mate is so weak in that area. Problems escalate when the stronger partner becomes critical of the weaker mate's inability to rise to the expected level of competency in that area.

Many husbands have expressed to me their disappointment at discovering the Cinderella they thought they married turned out to be one of the ugly sisters. The realization of their wife's imperfection causes some husbands to feel they were taken advantage of or somehow misled. Of course, the same shock happens to wives when, after the honeymoon, they realize that Prince Charming is a frog after all!

Let's face it: Marriage is an intimate disclosure of ourselves — psychologically, physically, and emotionally. As singles we were able to keep other people at arm's length and only reveal our true selves in degrees. Our total self was kept wrapped like a surprise package to be opened on the wedding day. And that's the way God intended it. Why? Because full and intimate disclosure requires a loving, accepting relationship that cannot be easily severed.

There's no nakedness like psychological nakedness. When you open your total self to your mate, your strengths — as well as your weaknesses — are exposed. In the early years of marriage, every week that passes uncovers another weakness. We assume that our mate is going to see all those weaknesses, overlook them, and love us anyway. After all, doesn't the Bible say, "Love covers a multitude of sins." *Surely, he or she will ignore my little imperfections and concentrate on my gifts and talents*.

Okay, so you married a sinful, fallen member of the human race — join the club. All of us "have sinned and come short of the glory of God" (Rom. 3:23).

Some spouses make matters worse by mulling over in their minds, *What if? What if?* No matter whom you marry, you could ask, "What if?" Nothing will destroy love like concentrating on your partner's imperfections and comparing her or him to Mr. or Ms. Perfect next door.

Instead of focusing on the weaknesses of your partner, accept them, make permission for them, and concentrate on your partner's strengths. Isn't that what caused you to fall in love in the first place?

The Bible instructs us to concentrate on the good things about one another: "Finally, brethren, whatever things are true, whatever things are noble, whatever things are just, whatever things are pure, whatever things are lovely, whatever things are of good report, if there is any virtue and if there is anything praiseworthy — meditate on these things" (Phil. 4:8).

The eight characteristics cited in this verse are all positive.

When a person tells me, "I married on a wave of love, and now the love is gone," I make this suggestion: "You can create love by concentrating on your partner's strengths and refusing to dwell on his or her weaknesses."

An engineer from our church was married to an outgoing, bubbly, choleric-sanguine who was all energy. Respected among the church women, she exhibited all the qualities a pastor looks for in a godly leader. She had a way of organizing events and getting the other women to go along with anything she suggested. I had great expectations for her.

I was surprised one day when her husband — a quiet, sober-minded, statistician engineer — came to me for counseling. I could tell he was uptight. When I asked him why he had come, he started spilling out his feelings about his wife. As he talked, my image of her became contaminated by the ugly picture he was painting. Depressed and disillusioned, I prayed silently, "Lord, what should I say to this fellow?"

Finally, I looked him in the eye and said, "You know it's really a shame you married such a lousy woman."

His back stiffened, and he said, "Well, now, my wife isn't that bad."

"Can you tell me anything good about her?" I asked.

He thought for a couple of minutes and came up with a positive characteristic.

"Anything else?"

"Yes . . ." he responded with another good trait.

"Anything else?"

As he started to mention a third attribute, a smile crossed his face. "LaHaye, I know what you're doing."

Sure, I was trying to take his magnifying glass of criticism off his wife's weaknesses and put it back where it was when he fell in love with her . . . focused on her strengths.

Everyone has strengths and weaknesses. Your feelings of love or disdain toward your mate will be in direct proportion to the amount of time you focus your thoughts and attention on the negatives. Some people are born critics — especially those with a melancholy temperament. That's why I told my engineer friend, "Throw away your magnifying glass and concentrate on the praiseworthy aspects of your wife's character."

The same thing is true about your partner. Concentrate on your partner's strengths, and never, never permit yourself to indulge in dwelling on their weaknesses. Certain flaws in your mate's character cannot be overlooked and need to be addressed. When your partner has a weakness that drives you crazy and causes real problems in your marriage, don't let it eat away at you. I suggest you talk about the problem, and openly and lovingly confront your mate. If nothing changes and you come to an impasse, let it go for awhile. Once you've pressed the issue long enough, don't keep bringing it up. If you constantly nag your mate, you will destroy your relationship and sabotage any meaningful discussions about other issues.

"What else can I do?" you ask. "It still bothers me."

Face the fact that he or she may be unwilling — or unable — to change at this stage of his or her life. There is nothing more you can do except talk to your Heavenly Father about the problem. Lay your burden down, and cast all your cares on Him. Commit the situation to the Lord, and give Him time to work it out.

Begin to pray consistently for the strengthening of your partner's weakness. Pray with deep humility, realizing that you are not perfect either. As you pray, the Holy Spirit may begin to convict areas in your own life that need changing.

Avoid criticizing your mate mentally or verbally. That does nothing positive. Praying does. You have probably heard the expression, "Prayer changes things" — and it does. It often changes the heart of the one who does the praying. At the same time, God will hear and begin to bring answers when you pray. Give God time to work.

Be Quick to Apologize

Men, don't be like the west Texan who moved to California.

Late one Sunday night, his wife called me and said ,"Can you come right over?"

They had just had a huge argument, and as I was trying to piece the facts together, she sobbed, "In the 24 years we've been married, he has never apologized to me."

I turned to him and asked, "Is that true?"

"Yep!" he replied, looking me in the eye.

"How come? Have you never done anything wrong?"

"Oh, yeah, I've done things wrong."

"Well, how come you never apologize?"

"Well, I don't think it's very manly."

This six foot four weight lifter — with muscles bulging out all over his body — is afraid to apologize to his 110 pound wife because it isn't manly.

I talked to him for a while, trying to get to the source of the problem.

Abruptly, he finally blurted out, "My pa never apologized to my mother in 30 years of marriage!"

"Just because your father made 30 years of mistakes, there's no reason for you to continue making them. Do you know what the Bible has to say about this?" I asked him.

"No," he mumbled.

"It says, 'Confess your faults one to another.' Do you know what happens when you confess? God reaches down into your wife's heart and pulls out what could become a root of bitterness." The more we talked, the more he realized the damage that results when one partner is too proud to ask forgiveness.

You can do something dreadful, but if you sincerely apologize — and your partner decides to forgive you — the Holy Spirit can keep that incident from being a tragedy.

Years ago, I made a terrible mistake that involved our two sons. In our community the garbage truck came twice a week, so I told the boys, "I'll put the full cans out on garbage days, and you boys bring them."

Now these empty plastic containers weighed only about five pounds. Week after week I reminded the boys, and week after week they forgot — or so they said. Once in a while they would remember, but not very often.

Finally, I said, "Now, fellas, I've had it! You're both big

enough to wrestle those trash cans, and when I get home at night, I want those cans put away." To help them remember, I gave each boy a certain day. "Now, Larry, I'm going to give you Tuesday, and Lee, you bring them in on Friday. And when I come home on Tuesday, I am going to hold you accountable Larry — and Lee you're accountable on Friday night. And if you don't have your trash can put away on your night, you're going to get a licking. Is that clear?"

I laid out all the ground rules, and they said, "Yep, we understand."

Everything went fine the first week, second week, third week. The fourth week, I came around the corner, and there were those trash cans on a Friday night. I marched into the house and asked, "Where are the boys?"

Bev answered, "Back in the bedroom."

I went back into the bedroom, grabbed Larry, turned him over the bed, and gave him a spanking.

As I walked back into the kitchen, my wife asked, "Honey, which boy did you spank?"

I said "Larry."

She said, "Oh. This isn't his day."

"You're right," I agreed sheepishly. "It's Friday."

Now what does a father do when he realizes that he has spanked the wrong boy? The first temptation I had was, "Well, it serves him right. Look at all the times he got away with it." Instead, I went back into the bedroom and sat down beside him on the bed. As he pulled himself together, I reached over and put my hand on his knee. I said, "Son, I understand I made a terrible mistake. This isn't your day."

He couldn't have agreed more, and then I apologized. I told him, "I was too quick. I acted in haste, and I am extremely sorry. Would you forgive me?"

I'll never forget the response of my ten-year-old son. "Oh, sure, Dad, that's okay. I know you're not perfect."

Years later, when he got out of the military and was married, he worked with Bev and I in our Family Life Seminars. During a seminar in San Bernardino, I forgot he was in the audience and shared the trash can story.

Later, Larry found me and said, "Dad, I don't remember that story. How old was I?"

As we talked, the light bulb went on, and he said "Oh, yeah, I remember."

Later, I said to my wife, "Honey, if I had not apologized to Larry that day, he would surely have remembered." Why? Because a root of bitterness would have wrapped around his heart and crippled our relationship for years to come.

I have never heard of anyone losing stature or position by honestly apologizing to a mate or to a child — but covering our sins can create permanent damage.

Apologize when you're wrong, and reaffirm your love. Simply saying, "I'm sorry," opens the door to a new start and allows you to put the incident behind you.

Verbalize Your Love

I received a sad letter from a wife whose 42-year-old husband was going through a time of uncertainty in his career and carnality in his spiritual life.

Suddenly, during one of their arguments, she blurted out: "You know, I don't think I love you anymore."

Her statement may have reflected the honest emotion she had at the moment, but she should have kept it to herself. Transitory feelings can be very deceitful.

Her husband started thinking about what she had said and decided he didn't love her either.

"Now we are living apart," she wrote. "We've only been separated for four weeks, and I realize what a fool I was. I really do love him."

My question to her would be, "Why did you let four weeks pass without apologizing and telling him how you really feel?" When we let too much time lapse between our expressions of love, negative emotions will rush in and fill the gap.

Over the years I have noticed that two temperament types have difficulty expressing their love: melancholys and cholerics.

Since cholerics are perfectionists — and almost impossible to please — they seldom feel that anyone is worthy of their love.

Usually a strong leader, the choleric often withholds affection or praise as a means of motivation — at least that's the way the choleric sees it. In an effort to challenge his or her mate — or kids, employees, students — the choleric sets high standards and waits for them to be met before bestowing love or commendation. As a result, those who live and work with the choleric constantly crave his or her approval. In fact, the more choleric you

are, the more other people desire your approval. Once you realize this, you need to look for opportunities to bestow that pat on the back or word of encouragement — and don't be afraid to say, "I love you" often and repeatedly to your family.

Don't expect everybody to perform as perfectly or efficiently as you do. Give others room to make mistakes — especially your mate and your children.

The melancholy person also has difficulty expressing love and affection. Why? Because he or she has a long checklist of 21 standards of perfection. If you're only a 20, the melancholy can't say, "I love you" today, because you didn't measure up. Instead, he thinks, *I'm sorry, but you didn't make the grade. Try again tomorrow.*

If you are a melancholy, you also set very high standards for yourself. That's why you're usually grumpy. Lighten up! Learn to enjoy life and other people. Give your mate a hug and say, "I love you," whether you feel like it or not. As you verbally express your love and physically show it, true affection will naturally grow in your heart.

We serve a God of love. He loves us and expects us to love one another. You may say, "She knows I love her. I don't have to tell her. I show it by the things I do for her."

Showing is good. In fact, "God so loved the world that He gave His only begotten Son." God showed His love for us by giving His most precious gift. Jesus also showed His love for us by willingly dying for our sins.

In addition to His acts of love, Jesus repeatedly expressed His love for His disciples — and for us — in words. "A new commandment I give to you, that you love one another; as I have loved you, that you also love one another (John 13:34). "He who has My commandments and keeps them, it is he who loves Me.

And he who loves Me will be loved by My Father, and I will love him and manifest Myself to him" (John 14:21).

When we withhold love from our mate, we disobey the commands of Jesus.

Years ago I appeared as a guest on the "Phil Donahue Show" to discuss my best-selling book, *The Act of Marriage*. At the end of the program — with 30 seconds left — Phil asked: "Dr. LaHaye, can you give me — in one word — the most destructive force in marriage? What causes marriages to break down most of the time?"

"One word? Yes, I can," I replied. "Selfishness."

It doesn't matter what temperament you or your mate are. If one of you is selfish in your relationship, you will destroy that relationship.

The Bible says, "Let each of you look out not only for his own interests, but also for the interests of others" (Phil. 2:4). Look out for whom? Others. An unselfish person is others-conscious.

In a marriage relationship, instead of looking at what the other person is doing to you — or has done to you — maybe you need to consider what you have done to your partner. Maybe you need to decide, *I'm going to treat my mate unselfishly.* Why? Unselfishness is love.

The 13th chapter of 1 Corinthians lists nine characteristics of love: Love is courteous, love is kind, love is generous, humble, patient, love has good temper, love is sincere, love is guileless, and love is unselfish.

Husbands, if you want to be loved by your mate, be kind to her. All a woman really wants is kindness. If you give her love and kindness, you will never have to worry about her being unfaithful.

God has given human beings the ability to transmit thoughts into another person's head by the vehicle of words. It's called communication. Husbands, your wife needs to hear you say, "I love you." In fact, God commands husbands to love their wives. How? "Husbands, love your wives, just as Christ also loved the church and gave Himself for her" (Eph. 5:25). God gave His "Word" to reassure us. He doesn't want us to be constantly wondering, Does God love me? Throughout Scripture, God communicates His love for you and me through words.

As a husband, you need to communicate your love verbally.

Why? To reassure your wife, to comfort her, and make her feel secure in your relationship. A wife — after five to ten years of marriage — will reflect her husband's treatment.

I have seen an insecure, fearful young woman from an austere, domineering family marry a loving, kind, and approving young man. After about five years, she's no longer an emotionally shell-shocked victim. Her friends look at her and think, *She's like a chrysalis out of the cocoon who has become a beautiful, uninhibited butterfly.* Why the amazing transformation? Her husband loved her. He not only showed it by his actions; he repeatedly and continuously verbalized it to her with words.

If your wife shows signs of being depressed, apprehensive, or on the verge of a neurotic condition, she may need a good dose of your unconditional love and approval. Husband, if you have used your tongue like a whiplash and cut her down and chopped her up into little pieces, you need to ask her forgiveness, tell her you love her, and change your ways.

"Love her, love her, love her, love her." Four times in Ephesians 5, this command is repeated. "Husband, love your wife!" Love her with your voice.

Try it, you'll be amazed at the result.

Be Thankful for Your Mate

The Bible says, "In everything give thanks; for this is the will of God in Christ Jesus for you (1 Thess. 5:18). Did you know the best way to perpetuate love in your marriage? Give thanks for your partner everyday.

In my years of marriage counseling, very few wives have told me, "I don't love my husband anymore." A women's love is elastic — it stretches — but a man's love is rather short and brittle.

One day, as I was having lunch with a friend, he began telling me that his love for his wife was gone. "I have no feeling for her," he said frankly. "In fact, we haven't shared the same bedroom for three months."

I don't know how it is where you live, but in California that's a sure sign all is not well.

After he finished talking, I looked at him and asked, "How would you like to fall madly in love with your wife in three weeks time?"

"Is it possible?" he asked suspiciously.

"Yes, sir."

"But we've been having problems for a long time, and it's just getting worse."

"I guarantee that if you do what I tell you to do, you will fall in love with her in three weeks." At that point, I reached into my pocket where I usually carry index cards. Taking one out, I said, "You've criticized your wife for 30 minutes, now tell me something good about her."

He thought for 10 minutes and came up with one positive point. And then another and then another. As he talked, I wrote down 10. Then I gave him the card and said, "I want you to thank God for each of those 10 things twice each day — every morning when you have your devotional time and then every evening."

He just stared at me.

"You said it takes 35 minutes to get from your office to your house," I continued. "While you're driving, I want you to pull out that card and thank God for those 10 good things about your wife before you arrive home. And in three weeks, you'll fall madly in love with her."

Ten days later, after the Sunday night church service, my friend and his wife came waltzing down the side aisle as everyone else was filing out. As they stood in front of me, he put his arm up on her shoulder, and she snuggled up next to him.

We exchanged a few pleasantries, and then they turned to leave. As she started out a little ahead of him, he turned around toward me and — in a stage whisper that could be heard out on the sidewalk — said, "Hey, we're back in the same bedroom!"

Indeed!

A couple of weeks later, I was going through the San Diego Airport when I had to call his office on business. When we finished our discussion, I asked, "By the way, how are things at home?"

He just about melted into the phone as he said, "Oh, it's super! Better than it's ever been before."

Suddenly, I realized that it had been three weeks to the day since we had first made the list. "Tell me," I said, "Do you have those 10 things memorized?"

He surprised me by saying, "Oh, I had those memorized the third day. But you know what I did, I turned that card over and wrote 15 other things I like about her."

If 10 won't do it, then you husbands may want to try 25.

This three-week guarantee has worked for many couples, but it does take some discipline. Not only must you thank God twice a day for the ten good things, you must also refuse to think anything negative about your partner. Once you train your mind to ignore the negatives, they become insignificant and fade away in light of the positive areas on which you are focusing.

Later, my friend's wife told me that when he came home the first two or three evenings, she couldn't figure out what was wrong. He was in such a good mood — and being so sweet — that she tried to smell his breath to see if he had been drinking.

This was quite a change from his previous behavior. As a choleric melancholy, his perfectionism had made him very critical of everything his wife did. In fact, she told me she had dreaded hearing his car pull into the driveway. "Oh, boy, this is where I get it. I wonder what I've done wrong today?" she would say.

About the fourth night, she was actually

looking forward to seeing him. His attitude had carried over and changed her, too. Love is infectious. So is criticism, hate, bitterness, and animosity.

Make sure that you thank God for your partner every day, and then expect God to bring about change in both of you.

Allow the Holy Spirit to Strengthen Your Weaknesses

Over the years, I have performed more than 350 weddings. Every couple I have married has one objective in common: Happiness. They think marriage is going to produce happiness. I don't try to tell them any different; they'll find that out soon enough.

If marriage doesn't guarantee happiness, what does? The Bible reveals the secret of happiness: "Blessed are they whose ways are blameless, who walk according to the law of the Lord" (Ps. 119:1).

What is the converse of that principle? Miserable are they who don't follow the laws of God.

Jesus said, "Happy" or "Blessed are they that hear the Word of God" and what? "Keep it." It's not enough to hear it — you have to keep it.

In John 13:17, Jesus said, "If you know these things" — the principles of God — "blessed are you if you do them."

You not only have to know the principles of God, you have

to do them. The good news is: We don't have to do it on our own. When you invited Jesus Christ into your life, His Holy Spirit came to dwell within you. He is your helper. You have His supernatural power within you to help you live the Spirit-filled life. When a natural human being is indwelt by a supernatural power, that person ought to be different. Right?

In what way should you be different? Has the indwelling Holy Spirit made you better-looking since you were saved? Did you get any smarter or more talented? I doubt it.

Your natural strengths may have been enhanced, but the Holy Spirit doesn't create any new physical, mental, or ability changes. So where does the change take place? In our emotions. The Holy Spirit helps us control our emotions. Look at the nine fruits of the Spirit. They all relate to areas of emotions that we — in the natural — are unable to control on a consistent basis. These fruit bring nine strengths into our life: "Love, joy, peace, longsuffering, kindness, goodness, faithfulness, gentleness, and self-control" (Gal. 5:22-23).

Every person is a composite of strengths on the one hand, and weaknesses on the other. If you desire to be strong in the Lord and in the power of His might, then seek to overcome your weaknesses by the infilling of the Holy Spirit.

Christian psychologist Dr. Henry Brandt defines a mature person: "A mature person is not a perfect person, but he is sufficiently objective about himself to know both his strengths and his weaknesses, and has a planned program for overcoming his weaknesses."

If you are mature, you need a planned program for overcoming your weaknesses. Fortunately, there is not a weakness in your life that cannot be fortified by one of the strengths of the Spirit-filled life. Once you identify your temperament type, you

can ask the Spirit of God to strengthen your weaknesses and bring your strengths under His control.

When you are filled with the Holy Spirit, you don't cease being your native temperament. You are what you are, and you will be that way for life. The Holy Spirit, however, acts as your helper to keep you from being driven or dominated by your weaknesses.

Let's look at several Bible characters whose temperaments were refined by the Holy Spirit.

Moses, the melancholy, was a brooder and a thinker. After all, anyone who could sulk for 40 years on the backside of the desert must have surely battled with bouts of depression. How, then, can a man at 80 years of age become one of the greatest leaders the world has ever known? He was transformed by the power of the Holy Spirit.

Moses — like all men — was not perfect. He still indulged in bitterness and hostility and died before his time because he never surrendered his angry disposition to God.

Moses was the only man who broke all Ten Commandments at the same time. In a fit of rage, he threw them down — and we've been using a second-hand set of Ten Commandments ever since!

Abraham appears to have been a phlegmatic since, in his early years, he was afraid of everything. God, however, changed him from a fear-prone wimp to a great man of faith.

The apostle Peter's behavior as revealed in the four gospels exposes an outgoing, gregarious extrovert — a definite sanguine temperament. Although he had leadership potential, his lack of discipline and self-control kept getting him into trouble.

After Peter was filled with the Holy Spirit he became a controlled extrovert. Instead of blurting out the first words that came to his mind, he began to think and engage his brain with his tongue.

The words Peter spoke and wrote — as recorded in the New Testament — were meaningful, uplifting, and helpful. His Spirit-controlled sanguine temperament enabled him to become a positive and effectual leader.

Saul's choleric temperament made him a raving religious zealot who — like a fiery dragon — was "breathing out threatenings and slaughter" as he tortured and imprisoned every man, woman, or child who refused to deny Christ. After he was

transformed by the Holy Spirit, the apostle Paul became a compassionate, tenderhearted leader in the early church.

God can change you, but He doesn't change your temperament or other personal characteristics. What does He change? Your weaknesses.

As you submit your will to the ministry of the Spirit of God, you will be gradually fortified with love, joy, peace, patience, kindness, goodness, faithfulness, gentleness, and self-control. The fruit of the Spirit will become the strength of our temperament — much to your mate's delight!

Decide to Walk in the Spirit

I'd like to ask you a couple of personal questions. Have you been walking in the Spirit in your home during the past week? How have you treated your partner and your children?

God's Word tells us: "If we live in the Spirit, let us also walk in the spirit." (Gal. 5:25). That's the key to marital happiness even if you and your mate are total opposites.

My wife and I try to walk in the Spirit most of the time, but it's not always easy. Since we are nearly totally opposite in temperament, we have different tastes in colors, in the way we work, and in our personal habits.

Bev is an early riser, and I'm a late night person. By 8:30 in the evening, she can barely hold her eyes open. I've learned not to ask her to do anything after 8:00 that requires a degree of mental alertness. In the morning, however, she's up, singing and happy. And me? I don't even know who I am.

I'm a very goal-oriented person. My motto is: "From production to perfection." If you're going to do something, let's get moving and do it.

Not Bev. She wants to get every detail lined up beforehand with all her ducks in a row. "From perfection to production" — that's her style.

Consequently, Bev and I have difficulty making decisions. If we both did not continually strive to live Holy Spirit-controlled lives, we probably wouldn't be married today. To God goes all the glory for the long, wonderful marriage we have enjoyed.

About three years into our marriage, when I was a church pastor — and Bev a pastor's wife — we were not happily married. If we had been asked to rate our marriage from zero to 100,

I would have scored it about 20. Bev was more generous — about 24. Today, we would put it somewhere between 100 and 110!

What happened to us? God the Holy Spirit changed us.

As a minister of the gospel, I had always depended on the Holy Spirit to preach and to bring people to Christ. Even in marriage, Bev and I sought the Holy Spirit's wisdom in the big decisions of life. When it came to our marriage, however, I knew nothing about walking in the control of the Holy Spirit at home. Yet, that's where "the rubber meets the road" in the Spirit-controlled life.

The apostle Paul, in writing to the Ephesian Christians, said, "Wake up! What's the matter with you? Stop acting like fools! Get your act together! Find out how God wants you to act!"

Actually, this is the way Paul put it:

Therefore He says: "Awake, you who sleep, Arise from the dead,

And Christ will give you light." See then that you walk circumspectly, not as fools but as wise, redeeming the time, because the days are evil. Therefore do not be unwise, but understand what the will of the Lord is. Awake you that sleep, and arise from the dead and Christ shall give you life. See then that you walk circumspectly, not as fools, but as wise, redeeming the time because the days are evil, therefore do not be unwise, but understand what the will of the Lord is (Eph. 5:14-17).

What is the will of the Lord? The answer follows in verse 18: "Do not be drunk with wine, in which is dissipation; but be filled with the Spirit."

What should Spirit-filled Christian husbands and wives be doing? "Speaking to one another in psalms and hymns and spiritual songs, singing and making melody in your heart to the Lord, giving thanks always for all things to God the Father in the name of our Lord Jesus Christ, submitting to one another in the fear of God" (Eph. 5:19-21).

The world in which we live knows nothing about having an uplifting song in their heart. All they know is how to be audibly inputted with headsets clapped on their ears or rock music blasting

out of their cars. Why? Because the emptiness of their lives can't bear silence.

Those who live without Christ don't know what it means to be grateful. We live in the most affluent culture in the history of the world, and Americans gripe and complain about everything and everyone — from the paperboy to the president.

And submissive? That's a dirty word. "No one's going to tell me what to do!" Everyone from toddlers to grandparents resists yielding their wills for the good of another. Rebellion is rampant, creating constant conflict at home, school, work, and in the streets. Why? Because people by nature are filled with self and not with the Spirit of God.

Let's look at the verbs at work in Ephesians 5:19-21: speaking, singing, making melody, giving thanks, and submitting.

Shouldn't Christians be different? Aren't we supposed to be doing the will of God? Think what a difference it would make in your marital relationship.

Husbands, how would you like to come home to a wife who's humming the latest praise tune while she's fixing dinner?

Wives, imagine your husband walking through the front door whistling the new chorus he learned at church last week?

What if the family's dinner conversation centered around the psalm you just read before blessing the food?

Wouldn't it be nice if before you went to bed at night, your husband said, "I'm so glad I married you;" and you replied, "You're such a wonderful husband. I don't know what I did to deserve you"?

Husbands, how would you feel if the next morning your wife told you, "I've been thinking about your suggestion that we cut back on spending. This month I've decided to color my own hair instead of going to the salon."

What if he replied, "That's great, honey. By the way, this weekend I can build that new flower box you wanted."

Are you trying to do God's will? Do you have a song in your heart? Are you cultivating a submissive attitude and a thankful spirit in your home? Are you living to please God and your mate — or do you only think about your own feelings and happiness?

If you answered "no" to most of those questions, you need to change. But you can't do it on your own. You need the power of the Holy Spirit at work in your life.

One day my phone rang, and a lady said, "My husband is a minister. Would you counsel us and keep our meetings confidential?"

"Of course," I replied.

As soon as I met the husband, I knew he was a hard-driving, energetic choleric. It was easy to identify his temperament since I am one myself.

"We've been married 22 years," the wife began. "And I've had enough of his angry outbursts."

"What happened?" I inquired.

"He had a tremendous fist fight with our 19-year-old son. My husband was cruel and brutal, so I left him — temporarily. I agreed to return home if would come with me for counseling."

I looked at him and said, "Sounds to me like you're a pretty angry man if these things are true. Are they?"

"Yes."

"Are you angry?" I asked.

"Well, Tim, you have to understand — a man has to have some place in life where he can relax and be himself."

Since I didn't know what to say, I was silent for a long time. Under the inspiration of the Holy Spirit, I shut my mouth and thought, *This very capable man is basically sincere.*

In the deafening silence, he got the message. Suddenly, he blurted out, "Gee, that sounds carnal, doesn't it?"

"Yes, it does," I replied. "May I suggest that when you relax and want to be your real self that you act with love, joy, peace, kindness, gentleness, goodness — that's the Holy Spirit."

"You're right," he replied meekly.

If you are not walking in the Spirit at home, you're walking in the flesh. When the apostle Paul said, "Walk in the Spirit,"

who do you think he was writing to? He was talking to born-again, former pagans — just like you and me. Many Christians tend to think that the Spirit-filled life is an option. "Do I want to be a Spirit-filled Christian or not?" they ask themselves. It's not an option — it's a command of God.

"I've tried," you say. "How can I walk consistently in the Spirit?"

Let me give you the same biblical formula I have shared with thousands of Christians.

First, examine yourself for sin. If you are indulging your emotions and giving into an area of weakness, you can change. Get this straight: You cannot walk in sin and walk in the Spirit at the same time.

If you have a pet sin, remember this verse, "Therefore we also, since we are surrounded by so great a cloud of witnesses, let us lay aside every weight, and the sin which so easily ensnares us, and let us run with endurance the race that is set before us" (Heb. 12:1). As a result of your inborn temperament, you have a tendency to sin in certain ways.

Some people have "the gift of criticism" — at least that's what they call it. Actually, they are critical people, and this sin is ruining their marriage relationship. Other people are undisciplined. Others are angry and cruel.

Some people are so passive, they are willing to sit back and let the world go by. These self-oriented, self-protected types avoid getting involved and simply let their mates handle every problem that comes along.

All of us have a tendency to fall into a sin pattern. You can be sure that Satan knows what it is, and he'll use your flesh and the world to tempt you every opportunity he gets. If you fall into that pattern, you cannot walk in the Spirit.

"How can I know what my sin pattern is?"

Every time you give in to some sin and the Holy Spirit convicts you, yield yourself to God and say, "Lord, is there some wickedness in my life?"

If you are regularly reading and studying God's Word and are open to hearing His voice, He will reveal the sin in your life. It will keep cropping up time and time again — in the pastor's sermon, in your devotional reading, on Christian radio — you won't be able to get away from God's convicting power.

Once you recognize the sin in your life, don't try to hide

from it. Face it — no matter how ugly it may be — and take the next step.

Second, confess your sin. According to 1 John 1:9, "If we confess our sins, He is faithful and just to forgive us our sins and to cleanse us from all unrighteousness." Claim God's forgiveness through the shed blood of Jesus Christ. It doesn't do any good to keep beating yourself over the head. Jesus has already taken your punishment on the cross. Accept it and thank Him for forgiving you.

Third, yield your total self to God. Many sincere people confess their sin after they've faced it, but they never take all the wraps off and give themselves totally and completely to God.

The Bible commands us: "Offer yourselves to God . . . and offer the parts of your body to him as instruments of righteousness" (Rom. 6:13). You will never be filled with the Holy Spirit until you unreservedly give yourself to God as His possession.

We are commanded to love the Lord our

God with all of our heart, all of our soul, all of our mind, and all of our strength (Mark 12:30). God tells us that He will not share our affection with another. He is a jealous God. He wants all of your heart — not 99.4 percent.

Are you willing to surrender it all and say, "Lord, if it's your will, I want to give you everything in my life. I want to give you all that I have and all that I am"?

In your mind's eye, visualize yourself lying on an altar dedicated to God. Pray: "Lord, I am 100 percent yours. I give you my total self."

If there is a habit, a thing, a person, or some specialty in your life that you have been unwilling to give Him, pull that up on the altar with you right now. Then say, "Lord, I give you that." Don't short-change yourself by holding back from God. Never be afraid of God. As you give yourself to Him, He will multiply and bless and enrich your entire life.

Fourth, ask to be filled with the Holy Spirit. Jesus said, "If you then, being evil, know how to give good gifts to your children, how much more will your heavenly Father give the Holy Spirit to those who ask Him!" (Luke 11:13).

Did He say, "Beg me," or "Tarry all night," or "Fast and pray"? No. "Ask," He said.

If you want to be filled with the Holy Spirit, meet His con-

ditions and ask Him. Being filled with the Holy Spirit is a command, and God doesn't make His commands hard. All we have to do is receive His indwelling, controlling power. If you've never received the Holy Spirit into your life, may I suggest you do so right now by asking Him to come in.

Fifth, believe that He's filled you with the Spirit. How do you know if you've been filled with the Holy Spirit? That is easy to tell. Just examine the life you live at home. If you have reflected the Spirit-filled life at home by the way you treat your spouse and your children, treating others with love and kindness out of a spirit of peace, that is the acid test.

If you have yielded yourself completely to God and asked Him to fill you with His Spirit, then trust Him that you are filled. Then thank Him for what He's done.

Sixth, enjoy life in the Spirit. When God fills us with His Spirit, He increases our joy, making us contagious to those around us. As a Spirit-filled believer, you will have a song in your heart, a thankful attitude, and a submissive spirit (Eph. 5:19-21).

Have you ever met a miserable thanker? I haven't. A person who is gratefully thanking God has a positive attitude about everything. When you're filled with the Spirit, you'll have a song in your heart, thanksgiving on your lips, and a submissive or cooperative attitude. Who wouldn't want to be married to a person like that?

Don't Forget Habit

Being filled with the Spirit is not a once and for all experience. It is a daily function, just like eating or drinking. We need to be filled with the Spirit regularly.

One woman asked, "How often should I be filled with the Spirit?"

I replied, "Every time you're not."

Every time you see old habits of the flesh like anger, sarcasm, fear, selfishness, or other activities emerge — face it as a sin, confess it, and ask for a refilling of the Spirit.

Always remember, God wants to fill you more than you want to be filled. And I guarantee you will enjoy the results! And so will your whole family!